Gold Pours

Library and Archives Canada Cataloguing in Publication
Title: Gold pours / Aurore Gatwenzi.
Names: Gatwenzi, Aurore, author.
Description: Poems.
Identifiers: Canadiana 2021022441X | ISBN 9781988989372 (softcover)
Classification: LCC PS8613.A8975 G65 2021 | DDC C811/.6—dc23

Cover Art: Sonia Ekiyor-Katimi
Author photo: James Adetoye
Editor: Britta Badour

Published by Latitude 46 Publishing
109 Elm Street, Suite 205
Sudbury, Ontario P3C 1T4
info@latitude46publishing.com
www.latitude46publishing.com

We acknowledge the support of the Ontario Arts Council and Canada Council of the Arts for the production of this book.

ONTARIO ARTS COUNCIL
CONSEIL DES ARTS DE L'ONTARIO
an Ontario government agency
un organisme du gouvernement de l'Ontario

Canada Council for the Arts
Conseil des arts du Canada

Gold Pours

poems

Aurore Gatwenzi

46

This book is dedicated to Jessica Ntahoturi. To our beautiful childhood memories, the growth we were allowed to experience together while you were here on earth. The city we grew up in, the motherland we both shared, our similar nuanced identities. We understood one another. I'm grateful I had you as a friend. I am enraged we lost you to the ways of the world, but our God is merciful, and you live on in our hearts. Rest in Paradise

I don't know how to cope,

You've left me with no hope.

Feel like I should have known

The pain that you have shown

Would lead you sad and torn

Now here we are to mourn.

- Grieving Jessica

Blessed are those who mourn, for they will be comforted.

Matthew 5:4

Table of Contents

If you abide in my word, you are truly my disciples, and you will know the truth, and the truth will set you free.

John 8:31-32

it must be pure and come
from within, it must ring
truth, it must be soaked
with earnest words

anything that isn't organic
will not suffice

the writer is the receptor
the writer is the instrument
of the truth

when you reveal the truth
you heal

poetry is not personal

thoughts while I bathe

I think it's difficult
to admit your imper-
fections to yourself

to be able to make
a poetic prose about them
write them down

I've been having a conversation
with my flaws, pushing back
the layers of my being

speaking softly to them

correcting them   with love.

reflection

about rain. about music

of raindrops

trickling down my rooftop.

my roof. mine. I have a rooftop.

I am sheltered. warm, covered, untouched.

still. the rain calls me

out to dance. the cold wet reminds

my body that it too can feel

every inch of who I am.

I am not only this soul.

no, I am also this body.

I get caught up in the chemistry

I forget that this vessel

this body

carried the weight for years.

I cannot discredit who I was and who I've become and who I will be.

in this body society would love to dictate how I feel.

so about rain.
droplets pounding
against my brown skin
like dirt
mixed with water
molding me muddy.
wash away the lie.
brown skin like clay
for I am the Potter's vessel
filled with authenticity.

droplets running. down my curves.
curves like valleys, shallow waters
fill me
rendering me barren.
wash away
the hyper. sexualization.
curves like hills
bountiful and tender

like the depth of my nuanced waters
my body. this body. this vessel she is

mighty. she is fierce, she is soft, she is sweet.
she feels intensely. rain.
I like to think of you
as God's tears
baptizing His creation.
made new. something about the rain.

leaves me absolved

she's not asking you to feel sorry for her,

she is telling you to respect her.

not a victim

the religion we have come to know
simply put is real life stories
of other people
from many years ago
on their journey to serving God

we follow through their paths,
learn from their experiences,
instill them in our lives.

this may be communion
sometimes narrow-minded
we use their practices and rituals
call it sacred
without any real connection with God
have you found your peace ?
have you found your purpose?
if not, question it!
make your faith stronger

you are on your path

this is spirituality

I'm very open and transparent in hopes that I will attract similar souls towards me. I like talking to people about themselves. to see how we can relate. I've been forced to see things from other people's perspective. from a loving and patient point of view. when I was little I was placed in an environment that I believe accidentally viewed me as "other" and so forth treated me as such. it was a disguise. so I watch people. and I have always watched people. I hear and most of all I listen. I empathize with how they feel. I put it into words for them. be as eloquent as possible. I've come to find that a lot of similar experiences are repeated. through everyone I meet. if you are triggered that's the point. out of fear, not willing to expose. naked and ashamed.

sound familiar?

how is it that my soul speaks
when my ego engulfs my feelings
poetry flows lightly
carrying my heavy burdens to You
you speak to me in my darkest hours
the light at the end of the tunnel
my head bows down towards my paper
the mighty pen puts feelings to words
I know this sentiment all too well

hallelujah. there is a God

My heart is like a well,

only filled from a pure

source deep within.

You may come by with your bucket

plunge it to see how much it can take.

Walk away when you think you've satisfied your thirst.

Know that you will not be quenched for long.

For what you seek was never truly me.

What you are looking for is the Source.

girl read your bible

precious treasure in a cave
brought through the fire
dirty to purity
melting and refining
like a cascade
unrestrained feelings
Gold Pours

Gold Pours
unrestrained feelings
like a cascade
melting and refining
dirty to purity
brought through the fire
precious treasure in a cave

gold pours

Start children off on the way they should go, and even when they are old they will not turn from it.

Proverbs 22:6

When I was a child, the newspaper
Had a kids section with activities
The one I preferred was connect-the-dots
You follow the numbers and dots and
in the end it creates a beautiful image.
I envisioned life like this.

I didn't follow the dots,
The image in the end was more abstract
Or maybe I did connect the dots?
Like I would so often as a child looking at the stars
Thinking I am so small
Those twinkling dots in the sky

We call them constellations
They are bright and incite creativity
Who decided that a group of stars
Could look like a big dipper ?
The imagination it must have took
to amplify that vision to spread that knowledge
The stars
They give us a vision

We wish upon them, give them meaning
Or maybe they give us meaning ?
Just ask the wise men who sometimes follow them
Stars they are light and they led us to light
Which is still beauty within itself.

I see the bigger picture now

When I was a little girl a hummingbird always came to our window to suckle the sweet nectar from the orange lilies that grew in our front yard. Hummingbirds make no noise.

They are swift, consistently in motion, colourful and beautiful. I love birds. I love their chants and their freedom. Soon I began to imitate them, a false imitation of course. I had no idea how to whistle. So I would play pretend as most children do. My uncle would laugh at me and taught me how to whistle like a real bird so I could speak to them. I began to whistle, they would never answer back. In fact they flew away. So I was left to my lonely devices whistling by myself. Enjoying the inner peace I felt whistling. I bet that's how the bird felt. Peaceful.

When I was a little girl, I had my first crush. His name was Moses. Moses was my first crush. Yes, "*let my people go*" Moses. I would watch The Prince Of Egypt everyday after school. Memorized the soundtrack. I told my dad when I grow up I want to marry Moses. He said OK. One day, he flew away to Lebanon on a business trip. He called me and told me Aurore, guess who I am standing next to? *Who?* I asked. He said, Moses. I was shocked! *Can I speak to him?* I'm not sure how the conversation went. I'm sure I was shy. This year my dad reminded me of my chat with my first crush. I could not stop laughing. Apparently, my father told the Dean of the Department of Religious Studies at the University of Beirut that I was *determined to marry Moses* and he said he would pretend to be Moses over the phone to humour me.

In my teenage years I had a new obsession. The feminist in me was awakening. Moses had a wife. When I found out he had a wife and she looked like me, I obsessively studied her story. She was black and discriminated against for her skin. God's wrath gave Moses' sister leprosy because of her racism towards her. All the literature I could find about her, I read. She and I were long lost sisters. Kindred Spirits. Tsippora. What does it mean? I needed to know everything about her. Bird.

A woman named after a bird is a woman named after freedom, a woman named after a melody, a woman named after peace. A woman like her was married to one of the first freedom fighters I ever admired.

freedom

it is said that she is cursed
that our common ancestor committed a terrible sin
but my dear look at her
she believed Him when He said, "It is done."
her very existence
she expresses love
she walks by
whistling to the rhythm of her heart
she dances to the rhythm of the drum
cadence is in her blood
the blood
that courses through her veins
is from the motherland
her heart beats so loud that she can't help but listen to it
delectable skin like chocolate, glistening,
the sun fills her with radiance as her melanin absorbs the light
giving birth to creativity that ignites a fire inside every soul she encounters.
gold pours out of her mouth riches ingrained in her soul
hair defying gravity resembling ethereal clouds
as her mind is reaching for paradise

this girl is blessed

inspiration fails you as your imagination sails right by you
through the vast possibilities of what could be
you are stuck in the state of a daydream without
accomplishing any real dream
feeling stagnant as life flows right by you

in your mind you're floating,
you are swimming, you are drowning,
you're splashing around.
but are you in a public pool?
shallow, man made, with no real depth.
where anyone and everyone can drive right in.
or are you on a private beach, soft sand,
salt water where the elite few can attend.

you should be aiming to swim in the ocean.
with a view as beautiful as the dawn
and a depth as deep as the Marianas Trench.
only a select few would dare to venture.
but darling you are not for the faint of heart.
you are here to be bold.
to dive right into the deep end.

trusting you could never drown no matter how tired you get.
you know how to float
your face will remain above water
so let's get wet, you want to be drenched.
we are baptized with our purpose.
this is where we will always belong.

I am christened Aurore, the dawn of a new day.
defined by grace I fear no obstacle.
courageous and young
my light brings warmth and novelty.
joyful and free, my days bring smiles.
the time has come for me to finally set sail.
I aspire to inspire those who come with me.
through the bridge of words I will emulate the feeling
of finding yourself whilst lost at sea.
I'll arrive at shore leaving imprints on the soft sand
And surely the water will keep kissing my feet
Tempting me towards the unknown
But I've found my way back in the land of the living
Until I set sail again.

here is where I'll stay

in my ancestors language my name is Gatwenzi
it means daylight smiling at you
it means dawn
it means laughter beaming like a ray of light
it means daybreak
it means novelty
it means let there be light

embodiment

I remain confident of this, I will see the goodness of the Lord in the land of the living.

Psalm 27:13

What is beauty ?

in the details...

meticulously curious

she speaks with her hands

so when they are carried to her chest

you know her Word comes from the heart

lovely & lively

curious stares begging to get to know you,
charming foreign men offering jewels, sweets,
conversational lush, knowledge.
strangers greeting you like family,
generous hands at any given moment,
warmth is not only found under the sun
it's in the hearts of fellow men.

travelling

The sun lies yet she also rises

let there be light.

To every disillusion there will be

epiphanies.

there is nothing new under the sun

I say a joke to see you smile,
It gives birth to your laughter
You are loud and beaming,
giving life to conversation,
And it feels like cotton candy
sweet and light.

what is your favourite emotion?

A new commandment I give to you, that you love one another, just as I have loved you, you also are to love one another.

John 13:34

it's difficult to not fall in love
with all the beautiful people I meet
artists are a different breed
they are out of this world and into their own
come and see

I'm an open book

Me: Do you ever look at faces? Just, like, in general, look at your face and think Hmm *this is what people look at when they see me?* Do you ever think of the importance of faces? Do you ever look at people's faces but see more than their face?

Her: I think about it all the time now because I found out there are so many people who can't form images in their mind of anything at all and if they're asked to describe someone they can't see the person's face in their mind so they describe them according to a list of (usually non-physical) facts. They recognize people but they can't think of their face if they aren't right in front of them. I think about the saying "Know you like the back of my own hand" and I'm like I'm not sure if I really know my hand all that well. And then I start obsessing over hand identities.

Every time I meet a new face, they look a certain way to me but depending on how our connection develops they start to look completely different from when I first met them but in reality they really look the same. My perception of their face becomes a result of their actual physical appearance plus my opinions on them or the nature of our relationship.

For example, I realized this when I was friends with this guy for about 4 years and then we started dating and his face started to look so much more beautiful to me and like a completely different person.

Me: That last part about getting to know someone and their face becomes so much more beautiful. It goes to show we are more than our bodies. Our souls do shine through.

Her: Yes absolutely. Language does this observation no justice.

Random guy listening in: It's love. *rolls eyes.

conversational lush part I

I love languages

they are bridges   to understanding

I love how we humans manipulate language

the accents   like spices

add flavours to a meal

it enriches the tongue

the way people talk

I want to know why you speak like that?

language betrays who you are

you can't hide with the way you speak

so speak to me

let me hear your language

I want to delight
in you

what flavour do you add to the mix ?

Him:

Self-reflection is never easy. It means questioning what you thought was certain. Imagine your whole life you thought the sky was red only to find out its blue, the courage you need to accept that you were living a lie and have to accept the reality of that. Taking responsibility for that requires great courage, a strong character.

Characters I fear we in general don't possess.

I don't think we know who we are, just know who we want to be. I'm trying to figure out what I am, which in part will let me know who I am. I know who I want to be. But maybe who I want to be requires accepting what I am.

My true self. But I often mistake my pure self which is my animal side as my true self. The true self is the only positive, the pure self is negative when connected to the true self brings out the positive sides of my pure self.

To be honest, as I get older, I realize my pure self needs control, of course I express it once in a while but it should be controlled and moderated.

The only way to survive is in alliance with the true self. The pure self cannot survive, it's destined to go back to its origin, the dirt.

conversational lush part II

sometimes people know how to manipulate situations
and like to play the antagonist
victim or hero
even the narrator of the story

you're none of the above
you're just a person living in God's world

find comfort in that

they should spark a light in the darkness

friends

Au. that is gold.
you know what silver is on the periodic table?
AG. like your initials Aurore Gatwenzi.
I was just destined to be a precious element.

gold is one of the most unreactive elements.
hm.. What does that mean?
it means you should be like gold.
no I know that's what you mean
but chemically what does it mean?
it means put it in water or hydrogen
it just is. It doesn't change. It's constant.
gold is just it's own thing

That's how you see me. It is true, I am my own thing,
but I do change.
my ability to change my mind is what makes me
human and good.
I'll keep Au. G. as a stage name
it sounds original and I do try to stay gold.

conversational lush part II

different readers will have mixed reviews of the same book.
a plethora of perspectives concerning the same story
an individualized experience of one tale.
people have their own walks of life
which affects their views, interests, ambitions, and beliefs
you cannot experience a book through the eyes of another
you are the author of your being

know yourself

How is it that the truth we know is the lie they live?
Everyday we wake up meeker than the rest by default
And it was told that we will inherit the earth for it.
We do. Chosen ones. We are not forsaken.
We take the time to understand fellow man as a means of survival.
And so we become servants to the people
This isn't something to be ashamed of
You are forming a bond, a connection, a greater interaction
love.
Speaking, listening, seeing from the heart
A servant is simply another word for leader.
So touch those you serve and lead with the truth you know
For this is what makes you great this is what makes you king.

service to humanity

Above all else, guard your heart, for everything you do flows from it.

Proverbs 4:23

No one can ever imitate

what is yours to create

i wrote this out of fear

look at you attracting flies like a pile of shit

to be fair honey attracts flies too

if only I had cultivated my own garden
stayed rooted to my soil.
stunting my growth I let you unroot me
naïve as I was I let you pick off my petals
as the game began one by one they fall

he loves me

but why can't you appease my thirst like the rainfall
only pouring out your insecurities onto me

he loves me not

enrobing me with your darkness
don't you know a flower needs sunlight?

he loves me

why aren't my roots intertwined with yours
like they do so well with earth
I ache for the nutrients of my land

he loves me not

how can you claim to love someone
when you have taken them away from their comfort

he loves me

ripping me from the earth in which I blossom
you put me in a box
leaving me thirsty and starving

where have the petals gone?
why isn't there one left?

he loves me not

scattered on the ground
look at the mess you've created
decomposing with my seeds
where you've left me is now my home
I will root my past experience
so that new life begins to bloom
from which I'll grow so much stronger
I refuse to wither away
still believing in my beauty
my seeds will prosper throughout this dry land
sweet tears making it fertile again
I'm going to keep working on this garden

deflowered

he was like a tornado and
I wanted him to sweep me up in his heavy wind.

I wanted to spin wildly in the midst of his destruction.

rip me to shreds I wanted to die for him.
and I did a little. I died for him when he spit me out.

and I hit the hard concrete floor.
a part of me died there.

but the rest of me laying on the floor is alive.
and waiting for the storm to end.

for the rain to come and wash away the pain.
for the sun to come and dry away my tears.
for the rainbow to appear and bring hope of better days.

it's not the end

so many seeds planted in my head
a garden is forming & it's not Eden
the grain of insanity buried deep within
it grows, it's burning, aching to be freed

talk less, do more, don't overthink, do more-

it’s too late. I’m going to water the seed.
it’s going to be fed. it’s going to be fed.
& soon I will be dead & soon I will be dead.

psychosis

I now understand that you do not know me.
you never did.
you knew my reactions to your manipulations.
I see you
trying to mold me into something
you want instead of accepting me
for who I am
my reaction to your feeble attempts were visceral
I've been resisting a forceful hand
so call me crazy because you are correct.
when I was with you that's all I could ever be
the constant fighting, relentless arguing
that is a girl vouching for herself.
you can speak ill of me
it doesn't matter because
you aren't really talking about me
you are talking about the monster
the one you were trying to create.

puppet master

they haven't brought their darkness to light

evil

he comes from a broken home

he was bound to break you too

forgiveness

I sometimes wonder what it took you

To float above the water facedown

And not come back for life

I picture you immersed, *still*

Not gasping for air, *peaceful*

Heartbroken to no end

My beautiful friend
I think your soul haunts the Ottawa River

Like it sank down to the bottom

Your last sacrament

Reverse baptism, anointing of your sick soul

My dad took the ferry the week you died

He hated it and cursed it

that river took one of our daughters

bring your grief to God

it is simply nostalgia

darkness to light

your glass was half empty
pouring out your insecurities
into my glass half full
now overflowing with self-doubt
you made a mess of a solid foundation

and I can't contain the pain

he says

you're not a delicate flower

you're a weed.

I tell him that is so rude

no it isn't

you can withstand anything

you're strong

you can thrive anywhere

he says
you're like water
can be so calm
then a wave of emotions
will overcome
sweep me away
you have violent tides

my tsunami

the times I have witnessed you

endure my frustrations

and feeling remorseful are the times

I knew I should have already gone.

I am not the girl you love.

I have yet to really love myself.

the breakup

I know what it's like to be loved
because of you
but I don't know what it's like to love
because of you

heart of the matter

I say

you are the tallest of trees
in the forest that is my mind
no matter the weather my mood swings
you remain fresh and green
when left in cold
the snow only amplifies your beauty
enduring the toughest of blizzards
the cold never bothers you
you are stable in this wild forest
the only one who could withstand my storm
you become stronger and tougher
wearing your name so beautifully

you are the evergreen

tell me,
how can you read me like a book
when you are clearly illiterate?
you can't even get through a sentence
without getting distracted
judging a book by its cover,
then flipping through pages
does not mean you *read* the book.
you see a book is like a whole new planet
and my dear I am a world of stories.
you gotta read me like the Holy book
because you gonna need the holy spirit to understand me.
I am a holy woman
wonderfully and fearfully made
let it be known
you could never even reach the climax of my story.
don't go asking around about me
this will only limit your knowledge of me.
if the previous reader couldn't get through me
what makes you think you can?
you'll never know how the story ends
you'll never know my origin

you might have read a chapter dear
but that doesn't mean you know me

analphabet

I saw it in her eyes when she said your name.
innocence.

like a coursing river, peace reigns all around her.
calming.

like the deepest of rivers her silence is gold.

i am the mistress

eventually the tears dried out
I surprisingly grew nevertheless
he said, you're a weed
you can thrive in whatever environment.
and once again I was plucked.
but this gardener did *something* different
this time held onto my roots.
he put me in a pot and surrounded me with new soil
watered me when I was wilting
he was patient with me,
he cared for me,
gave me space to grow at my own pace
he guided me,
made sure I was facing the Son.
I had never met a gardener so careful.
I felt like I could grow.
he fed me truth although
flowers don't belong in a pot.
they need to be in the wild.
attract insects, provide sweet nectar

for more seeds to be sown

you cannot shield me forever
I cannot always be lifted up on high
you were taught to do everything for
the ones you love but what about you ?
I call you my evergreen
your foliage covered in snow
is like the weight of this cold world
on your shoulders
sparkling in the sunlight
it is beautiful
how much the branches can sustain
I am reminded that sometimes they snap

and you are only a man

will you still want me
after you find out
who I am or who I was
will you judge me for my past
(please say no)
I want to give this a go
I like this idea I've concocted of you in my mind
I think you like yours of mine
do you want to see if our puzzle pieces match?
do they complete the image like we feel it could?

the games we play

I know that I want to care for you
I do
the very thought of it makes me melt with desire
I know what I want..
without a doubt you occupy my mind, clouded...
I want you.
I think you like that too much
I know you've spotted me.
eyes narrowed grinning.
it's too easy.

you could drive me crazy

he asks

why do you pull away from me when I'm inside you?

coming together with you

is like having all the women you have hurt prior to me

their pain

suffering

angst

tears, *sweat*

the lies they believed

the stories you tell your friends

the fake laughs you shared

you are in love

with the idea of hurting a woman

more than the idea of you giving her pleasure

yet here I am

conquered

you know what I hate?
when we start reading books
then we get a little lazy.

we skip through sentences,
then pages and whole chapters
then get surprised when the story no longer makes sense
and ultimately decide to stop reading the book altogether.

the story of us

innocence is gone--

I guess.

friends convincing you to waste time on women who won't be your wife.

playing with hearts. playing with lives.

changing the course of a path.

once narrow, now wide.

the abundance of choices isn't the sweetest of fruits.

the greed is poisonous, perverting the mind

forming bonds only to break them

we live for the drama.

that's what we're good for.

we don't deserve peace.

they say nothing lasts forever but that's not what I was taught.

mere mortals, everything grows, changes, evolves in love.

and in love I want to rest.

because I was taught that it lasts forever.

and this is who I want to be.

eternally

don't you observe human behaviour?

nothing is sacred anymore.

there is no soul to tie with

the boy who gives his body away

to any girl who wants his seed.

you didn't love him.

virginity isn't even sacred.

I was taught this lie.

it's only sacred if you both make love for the first time together.

sex is only sacred if you both love one another.

you can only build soul ties through love.

don't lose yourself to the world

you scared him

my love is like woe

to be sweet, to love

I want to be good to you, care for you.

I want to please you.

to the figment of my imagination

the one I've concocted of you

after I've indulged your many lies

the mind games.

they say the heart is deceitful

but what good is a heart if it's not meant to feel passion.

our souls tied without touching.

in my mind that is.

I'm not too sure what's real and what is fiction anymore.
my head was in the cloud of smoke you'd heavily blow in my face.

I breathed in the toxicity happily.

who needs oxygen.

nothing even mattered. I hadn't felt this high in a long time.

longings, cravings, restlessness, sleepless nights.

I've come to the conclusion that this was not real.

it wasn't real.

it couldn't be it was all in my head.

thanks for the lesson

smokes and mirrors

I get lost in euphoria
pick the flavors
sensations
evoked within.
I am emotional
the feeling of excitement
hinders my taste of discernment

i like to sit with my feelings

we build people up
to the point where they start to think
they are God's gift to the earth
and they need to be praised
whereas sometimes we build
people up in vain
we forget
we're supposed to give it to God

we need to be humble

he didn't break your heart
he broke your ego

daddy lessons

my father was a freedom fighter.
his pen was his sword.
books burnt, mouth shut.
he left the country but it never left him.
residue of the strife in his heart
he came to this safe haven.
only to write more about the motherland
that had cradled him as a means to wean.

here lies the secret pieces of him

there is no right or wrong

there is only truth

I know we were meant to be
for a moment.

nothing lasts forever

I told my friend Heaven is a place where you and I
can be together.

she said don't insult Heaven like that

I have been gallivanting with my girls,

we're a bit lost but at least we know it

the freedom that comes with excess

is not freeing   it is dampening

my soul is tired

I go to this party

and run to God

I go to that party

and run to God

I am at a Party and talk to God

every saturday night out results in a day with repenting in church sunday.

I am the girl at the bar

witnessing

to the girl crying in the bathroom stall

I say the only man that will not break your heart is Jesus

the cab driver with the cross hanging from his rear view mirror

knows all about me.

I ask him if he believes in Christ

drunk.

my friend shouts I believe in myself,

as I laugh and shout I can't believe in myself.

I'm so lost I need Jesus.

that gave him quite a laugh.

this is blasphemous but

do you think God hears drunk prayers

I mean they are sober thoughts and

it really is the truth that spills out when I am

under the influence of this serum

and I can't help but always turn to

God whenever I'm inebriated off of anything

and I don't know why but I'm always directed towards him
when I'm high

I just sing out his name or start to pray...

and I don't know why I can't ever self medicate without
thinking about Him

and how he fills me or fills us or fills everything

life is just so full of God everywhere.

I am in awe. Of him.

Drunk off of him, high on him.

naturally... or forcibly

omnipotence

"oh the girl who speaks in metaphors,

yeah, she crazy. she casting voodoo spells,

incantations, don't fall for her charm,

deceitful, divination, she's a witch, a Jezebel, it's sinful,

she thinks she's the sun because the world revolves around her,

so self-absorbed, always trying to prove a point"

misinterpretation after misinterpretation.

let me give you my Word:

I am the tipping point like the dawn.

no, in fact she dreams of the Queen of Sheba,

riddle me this! Riddle me that!

she'll keep you on your toes, you'll be coming for more.

she's perpetually deep, yet she is walking on water.

ridiculously sweet like a baby, she is breathing underwater.

"she slept with him and this guy too, I feel responsible she is doing this because of me. You need to know yourself!"

purity is a state of mind not what lies between your thighs.

I understand this, do you?

I have agency over my sexuality DO NOT SPEAK OF IT for that is my vow of Chastity.

you still on that reckless protect your flower bs?

some are trying to cage you, own you, they see you as property.

others truly value you, want to protect you, keep you sheltered, kind and loving.

the world it's so bitter, do not love it.

we need to keep you sweet. don't bite the fruit if it isn't ripe.

I'm just saying,

some of you are ironically proud of your modesty and it shows...

child, in this perverted Western World?

different struggles, let's get real.

can these so-called men uphold the same standards for themselves?

do they think of this while they're busy planting seeds of insanity in your mind?

reverse psychology is such a slut, y'all she easy.

let me use it to my advantage too. Wake up, wake up.

she understands that she is in fact deeply human,

she loves the use of language,

after all at first there was the Word,

she lives for the very breath of God,

her face commands attention like Esther,

it hurts to look. "Big eyes...luscious lips... if I could just get one kiss... "

"exotic" They say...

I'm the original woman

I'm black and I'm proud.

sometimes I slip up but I know myself.

"she is always talking about racism, sexism, ableism, homophobia etcetera etcetera..."

when you've got the face the "God's" agree they want to see,

you should know my purpose is to intercede on behalf of those who won't speak up.

after all the world does not revolve around me...

I give to service humanity not because I'm stupid.

"perhaps she should go about it more gracefully"

but y'all wanna act like you can't hear me?!

let me flip a table or two, whip some sense into you.

too busy placing tares in my wheat field

I'm trying to give you life baby ugh why do I love you...

"she talks too much about her problems everybody knows she's got issues..."

don't we all? Don't you see the cross on my neck? The sins I wear them so blissfully, carefully, knowingly... I know who I am. Do you?

she probes the mind, intoxicated with wisdom, she seeks knowledge, iron sharpens iron.

she gives life, revives you in your weakest moments, she's not just SOME girl.

"always quoting the Bible, no wonder she doesn't make any sense, I hope she gets run over by a car"

cue exit* rolls eyes.

I really should have listened to my pastor...

she blessed and highly favoured and she knows it

you are under the guise
that I may leave myself for you
that because I've confessed my feelings towards you
I will abandon myself.
your wish is my command...
who do you take me for ?
my oh my... you do not know me at all
after all the time we've spent getting to know one another?
I am not the girl you use for an ego boost.
dear boy, I only loved you because I knew how to love myself first.

i know how to walk away

the distinct smell of nicotine brings me back to you.
I used to hate the smell of cigarettes,
I used to know that where there is smoke there is a fire
silly girl I walked right into it and let it consume me happily
and you stupid boy, you lit a fire in the forest that is my mind
a fire that will never die, this fire burns wild destroying everything in her path
ashes to ashes, this fire she purifies
ashes to ashes, this fire lights the trail I am meant to follow
ashes to ashes, this fire becomes me
I'm basking in the heat of the moment
I am on fire, but I am not burning.

I am warm, I am brilliant, I am passionate
ashes to ashes everything must come to an end
and so here we are...
I've almost forgotten what your mouth felt like against mine,
to be clear in this haze of every single memory I have of you
I remember that it only happened once
your lips were tentative and tongue a bit rash
maybe unaware of what to do with it ?
I could feel it in your touch...

I mean you're the type of guy who puts your hands on a woman's waist while kissing her.

I don't even remember how I got so caught up

you were careful, subtle, nervous. *humble.*

a novel effort.

I can't put my finger on it.

this is by far the worst kiss I had ever experienced.

and here I am still thinking about it a year later

you are the worst, I mean by a mile the most annoying creature I have ever come across.

you had the audacity to wake up the childlike nature in me!

And so today

I choose to remember the good, I choose to see things for what they were.

you are the best mistake I have ever made.

you are a boy, a young man ?

a stranger that's not really a stranger

but let's pretend to be for God's sake

we both know he is laughing.

shall we kiss on it ?

I do not sleep   I dream.

I do not live   I exist.

you haunt my dreams
I wake up tired

my thoughts keep jogging
restless
you
wrestle with my mind

stolen glances satiate my heart abundantly
I am reminded of how
I have always wanted to love like God
far away, unattainable
so close, if only you reach out.

engorged with words I can't say
I will let my eyes do the talking
awkward. discomfort. unease.   desire.

i can't wait to never speak to you again

it hurts me to deny how I feel.

I block access to my love

I love being myself -   free

I've never had to deny loving someone or something.

Now that I have to, I feel like a fraud.

i'm suffocating

you used the good in me
as a means to see the worth in you
then left me
now I do the same with the Almighty
and I'm sure
this isn't how it's supposed to work

irresponsible

do you ever start to worry that you don't feel as much?

did you become stronger with time because your feelings weren't as palpable

or did you become weaker because your feelings were not as potent?

how do you feel ?

the truth is I'm tired.
I spend days in my head.
daydreaming up fake scenarios
I'm stuck in my head.
everywhere I go.
I'm stuck with myself.
sometimes I don't like myself.
I care too much.
I love too much.
I am too much.
I act blasé.
I pretend I am chill.
I'm none of these things.
I want to be okay with loving.
I want to be okay with caring.

but I'm not

did you see her today ?

yes.

yeah you're always happier after you see her

the past - blooming love

did you see her today ?

yes.

it must be hard to see her everyday.

the present - wistful love

things are different now

I still think about you all the time
too much
I am afraid of never feeling that sensation again
you brought me hope
my goodness I was in love
and now I see you almost every day -
in my dreams your face shows up
as a subconscious reminder of unconditional love

I walk towards you every time
knowing it's just a dream.

I see you every time
in my head
my heart aches for you
but you don't want me
you never have
do you remember how you told me
you would still make an effort
once you were gone, to speak to me
I am laughing now,
the reality hits even more
it was one of the best lies I ever bought into

however, tread lightly,
with the next object of your desire
us creatures you love so much deserve the very best

we can finally put this all to rest
what I want for you is not me
what you want for me is not you
I will never regret loving you
only losing sight of me.

I deserve someone that can take care of me
and that someone is me.

distance made my heart grow fonder
of me, that is.
I lost you but at least I found me.

now every time I see you
all I'm reminded of is
remember when you fell in love slowly?
and that's the way it should be.

thank you for the memory
thank you for the feelings
thanks for letting me know

it is still okay to live with my heart wide open

I can't despise the one
that cracked my heart wide
filled it with love I didn't know could be.

I wonder if all the love I felt for you
will ever find its way back to me.

where does love go when it isn't reciprocated

I created a world compiled of our moments.
the hidden ones, the words that were left unsaid,
the stolen glances, the light touches, the outright banter,
the shared secrets, the stupid laughter.

I lift you up and show you your worth.
if I could, I'd love away all your misery.

don't you see what I see?
let me show you who we really are.

he said there is so much *more to life than this.*
and spiraled the confusion,
the tears I still cry after a year,
the danger of fantasy, the fit of drama with no comedy,
the people that got hurt, the person I became in the process,
the rage, the anxiety, insecurities resurfacing,
being left alone in a place I never wanted to be,
being led astray, feeling cheap, stupid, so full of hate,
hastily looking for instant gratification...

losing sight of who I am supposed to be

being self aware of your flaws
and self-abasement are different things.
when you can't find your qualities or
what your talent is and what you are
good at you have gone overboard.
you're not aware of your flaws,
you feel you are entirely made out
of them without any redeeming factors.
not true. find your light, let it shine.
there is a fine line between being humble
and having low self-esteem.

never mistake the two

you can be there for someone
without feeding into their delusions.

be compassionate to be yourself

you loved to romanticize being in the eye of the tornado.
because in the midst of chaos you are untouched.
but to leave the eye you have to move with the mess.
let yourself be swept away in the whirlwind.
land hard on solid ground.

you are in the clear

She is clothed with strength and dignity; she can laugh at the days to come. She speaks with wisdom, and faithful instruction is on her tongue.

Proverbs 31:25

no light in this world is brighter than the sun.
everyday it brightens every corner of the world.
the sun serves us.
it gives us incentive to rise.
that is why it dictates our days.
you see, you need to serve others to be a good leader,
the way to increase your value is to value someone else.

rise by lifting others

She is not lost my dear

She is multifaceted

Picasso, art,

She is the journey she lives

complete and ever changing

darling, She is growing

She is seeing new beginnings everywhere

She is the tipping point

trust me she is the change you want to see in the world

complex but never complicated

nuanced and at peace

she is as resplendent as the sun
when she rises rest assured so will you
she will plant a seed
in the garden that is your heart
and with her touch precedes warmth
where she shines
you will be nurtured
with her words that inspire growth
she is not easily accessible
up high head in the clouds
you can see it in her piercing dark eyes
do not mistake them for black holes
because they will swallow you whole
you may find yourself lost in her
I know its enticing, to touch the sun
but you should know to never chase her
it's an impossible task to accomplish
and if you get to close

she might burn you

she is like sand
a little bit rocky, nevertheless soft
she likes to be given the freedom
to get carried away
you can't have a tight grip on her
she will seep through your fingers
hold her up with the palm of your hand
admire her
how she moves with the wind

love her enough to let her go

she is a diamond in the rough
she reflects and can only be broken by another diamond
if you don't see yourself reflected in her light
it's because those who don't make sense to you
are simply not for you

stay in your cave

she hides her pain behind harsh criticism
she causes strife where it is unnecessary
art.   she may not understand it
she prefers to be realistic
live in the quote on quote real world.
Unaware that being immersed in art
is the truest of feelings.
art imitates life,
                              that imitates art,
                                        that imitates life...
does she know that she suffers like art?
curious, I don't think I like her
but I still love her

bittersweet

she has flowers in her eyes

nectar in her tears

connection to her roots

She is heaven on earth

Martha

a girl I once knew...

Jesus said to them, "A prophet is not without honor except in his own town, among his relatives and in his own home."

Mark 6:4

the country

I call home
has as many faces
as I have seasons.
sometimes you feel them all
within a day.

temperamental

come winter
the snow
will wash
away
the mess.
the water
purifies
even when
it's ice
cold

like my demeanor

If you google “city of Sudbury crater” a pot hole appears
What an analogy for this beautiful city.
Isn’t it funny how a meteor crashed and formed
Sudbury
Like an angel might have fallen from heaven.

Too much pride, you may have had
For your city and sometimes you have it for you.
This city that wouldn’t exist without explosions
I’ve had my share of outrage here
Feeling imprisoned
This soil is acidic.
Bitter but capable of extracting sweet fruits
Blueberry.
Blue baby.
That’s how it gets sometimes during the winter.
And white, oh so white...
Yeah, we’re not just talking about the people.

I am from the north
Though my face is from the east
And my skin is from the south
I am from the north.

Cold.

Like the mines

What builds this city,

What built my character

I'm a miner searching for gold

I keep ending up with pyrite

Fools.

When I discover lost treasures

I am so relieved.

Aaaaaye

Mining is laborious, draining I'd say.

Sometimes you're left in the dark
With no jewels to save face.

And I know here that there are traces of gold.

Like the fact that this city turned a mess into a masterpiece

That old hospital ain't haunted

It is enchanted.

This city is a crater, she got depth.

And if you can't see it, find it in yourself.

Because this city made me

It's where I grew up.

She rejects me.

It’s where I have my fondest memories

She is deep. She is deep.

God is within her, she will not fall

Sometimes you forget about yourself...

How many explosions will you keep causing and deterring?

How many ?

There's nothing left, you have to resurface.

the mines were a very dark place

Mother says: "the idea is not to become cold my dear
but be cool and beautiful. Look how the snow covers
the branches wonderfully; they bend yet they never break.
As should you."

word from the wise

And when she has found it, she calls together her friends and neighbors, saying, 'Rejoice with me, for I have found the coin that I had lost.' Just so, I tell you, there is joy before the angels of God over one sinner who repents.

Luke 15:9-10

there are 2 sides to a coin.
have you ever tried keeping one upright?
it's much easier to lay it flat on the table
but it can stand if it's balanced.

understanding dualities

thorns protect a rose

experiences protect my being.

although they are painful it doesn't mean

that nothing beautiful can stem from them.

flourish

Frankincense and Myrrh in the air walking through church doors feels like peace after putting lotion on my skin after a long hot bath.

.Baptismal.

I fold my hands like a prayer and rub them together building heat, like the candle's flames at the altar massaging through every inch of me moisture enters my flesh, like the holy spirit enters my soul.

.Revitalizing.

As I always feel after speaking with the Almighty my body is His temple I will treat it as such so that my skin glistens looking like bronze in the heat cloaked in white seated in the pews I listen and heed the homily is the seed that sprouts in the garden that is my mind you can tell by my wooly hair, looking like celestial clouds.

.Ethereal.

I am in the world but not of this world the Word grabs a hold of me cradling me like the warmth of my mother's womb

.Genesis.

I am reminded that I've never been afraid of the dark because I am the light falling to my knees, my tears salt the earth my heart lights the world mind, body and soul what a miracle.

God.

made me beautiful

laughing happily
loving carefully but fully
kissing slowly, passionately, intently,
touching longingly, attentively, excitedly, wildly, wholly
I mean *holy*
feeling
divinely,
awfully sublime.
Masculine. Feminine. Energy...
immersed, Separately. Intertwined.
it is good.
desire

bring me to my knees

The love you have for me is transformative.
You are a mere mortal here I am, raptured by your affections.

The love you have for me is challenging.
To be reckless with your heart is wicked and shameful.

The love you have for me fills me with peace
It's not obsessive or possessive.
It's sensible, caring, free, calm, secure.

The love you have for me is gracious
When I wound us you kiss my scars before yours.

The love you have for me is secure
If I ever leave you and I come back to you

I pray this love won't vanish
I pray I haven't made you insecure,
I pray I haven't given you a complex

The love you have for me is forgiving, understanding
I feel no issue surrendering

Because you love God.
More than you love me.
More than you love anyone.

The love you have for me is not for me, it is for God.
I will not surrender to you but to Him

The love we built can never crumble
It is built on a solid foundation.
I think the God in me found the God in you,
and decided to pursue the God above.

We have taken a hold of heaven and refuse to let it go
We are not in love. We are IN love.
We have not fallen in love.
We have loved, are loved and are loving.
This is the holy trinity.

we are called to express love

The sunlight grazes
through the shutters of my window
bouncing off the reflection of my mirror
and onto your sleeping face.

Light.
It has a funny way of doing that.

Slipping through cracks, mirroring
                                        your beauty
I observe
the specks floating
How can such minuscule, irritating,
(dare I say useless)
particles reflect such a dazzling
Dance ? Slightly, up and down
moving and still.

Accumulating space,
Beautifully
Kind of like you and me.
And US.
In this moment.

Quarantined.

We are moved.
By the kindness of a stranger
By the generosity of neighbours
By the service of workers
By the support of healers
We are moved
By all the connections

Feeling helpless at the impending doom
Seeking God,
we are asked to take our Sabbath
God says *come sit with me.*
Basking in His light.
Take the time to reflect
Shine a light on the next
God is the light we are the dust.
Dancing in His world.
Reflecting His love on one another
at ease but not quite.

my god look at us.

Notes

I choose to separate this book by bible verses that the poems I wrote emulate or shed light upon. The section that speaks about love, heartbreak and God has to do with guarding your heart and is also the biggest part and lesson of the book. As I said my heart bleeds on these pages.

The book is called Gold Pours because of the feeling of being in the dark gone through hell and having been broken so many times but filling the cracks with gold is beautiful… to make that happen gold goes through a process… melting and refining is building character to fill my cracks… my cracks are the unrestrained feelings pouring out into poetry. Poetry is gold kind of like the quote from the outsiders saying to stay Gold meaning to stay innocent, true to yourself, unphased.

Gold Pours. I will stay Gold despite the hardships… That's precious.

Acknowledgement

Thank you to Heather and her team at Latitude 46 for believing in this project and putting my book out into the world.

Thank you Britta for picking and laughing at my work helping me see things from a different perspective during the long editing session the book would not have been the same without you.

Thank you to my parents, for instilling reading and writing in my heart from a young age .

I don't know why I feel the need to thank my first-grade teacher Mme Nathalie that I will never forget because she taught me how to read and she remains my all time favourite of all.

Thank you to my friends, who have supported me from the beginning. I wouldn't be here without your words of encouragement.

Thanks to past lovers for breaking my heart and filling my heart with more love than I could ever imagine as well. You are a part of this journey

And of course, I must thank the Most High. Give Him praise. I remain in love with God and find freedom in his loving embrace. Thank God for life, and books and love.